Henri
Rousseau

Henri Rousseau

Doreen Ehrlich

PRC

This edition first published in 2001 by
PRC Publishing Ltd,
8–10 Blenheim Court, Brewery Road, London N7 9NY

A member of the Chrysalis Group plc

© 1995 PRC Publishing Ltd.

ISBN 1 85648 625 7

Printed and bound in China

FOR BEKAH AND DANNY

PAGE 1:
*Liberty Inviting the Artists to Take Part in the
22nd Salon des Indépendants* (detail), 1906
Museum of Modern Art, Tokyo

PAGE 2:
Myself, Portrait-Landscape (detail), 1890
National Gallery, Prague

Contents and List of Plates

Introduction

The ironies and contradictions in Henri Rousseau's life, art and reputation are many. Even the nickname by which he is generally known, "Le Douanier Rousseau," is misleading, as Rousseau worked in a humble capacity as a *gabelou* in the municipal toll service from 1871-93. His job was to check on the duties payable on goods entering Paris and he never attained the rank of Customs Inspector or *Douanier*. The term appears to have been used in the artist's lifetime by Rousseau's first biographer, the radical poet and critic Guillaume Apollinaire, as a sign of the affection in which the painter was held by such avant-garde contemporaries as Picasso and Gertrude Stein, whose origins and lives were so different from his.

Beginnings

Henri-Julien-Félix Rousseau was born in the town of Laval in northern France, in 1844, which makes him of the same generation as Claude Monet, born in 1840, and Paul Cézanne, born in 1839. Rousseau's father was a tinsmith and hardware dealer, and the family lived in one of the two picturesque fifteenth-century towers known as the Beucheresse Gate. Rousseau was educated to secondary school level, which was unusual at the time, but his family were thrown on hard times and suffered a steep decline in social status, when his father speculated his money and was declared bankrupt in 1851.

The family moved to Angers, where the young Rousseau was employed in an attorney's office. Here he seems to have attempted some petty theft, stealing stamps and small sums totalling no more than 25 francs, for which offence he was brought to trial. In December 1863, it appears that Rousseau enlisted in the army, partly to escape the consequences of his action by appearing in infantry uniform at his trial, although in the event he received a month's prison sentence. This period of his life is clouded in mystery, much of it of Rousseau's own making. The early petty theft remained hidden, even when Rousseau was brought to court on a related but more serious charge in the last years of his life, almost 40 years later. On the second occasion Rousseau's paintings were brought to court in his defence, as proof of his innocence and gullibility, and he was given a suspended sentence, although he had to serve a period of imprisonment while awaiting trial.

In later life, Rousseau maintained, to such young admirers as Guillaume Apollinaire and the radical poet and playwright Alfred Jarry, that he had served as a regimental musician in Mexico, had risen to the rank of sergeant, and saved "the city of Dreux from the horrors of civil war." The facts would appear to be that Rousseau never left his native country, but served four years as a private in France, obtaining his discharge in 1868. Army records describe his appearance at the time: "height 5'4" (1.65m), oval face, high forehead, black eyes, average nose, average mouth, rounded chin, dark auburn hair and eyebrows, cut on left ear."

That Rousseau retained a nostalgic memory of his army service is implied by the tales he told his young admirers, in which it seems likely that he was not beyond appropriating the experiences of others as his own. In the barracks at Angers he may well, for instance, have heard soldiers' tales of the ill-fated French army expedition to Mexico in 1867, to install the Austrian Archduke Maximilian I as Emperor of Mexico, which resulted in Maximilian's death by firing squad. Apollinaire, in a review of the Salon des Indépendants in April 1911,

BELOW LEFT: The banks of the Seine and the Pont Neuf in the 1860s, when Rousseau was working as a toll-collector.

BELOW: Toll-collectors at work in the late nineteenth century.

BOTTOM: Rousseau in his studio in the rue Perrel, c. 1907.

stated as fact that "Rousseau had taken part in the Mexican campaign, and his poetic and plastic recollections of tropical vegetation and fauna were most precise."

Rousseau's knowledge of army life, and his continuing fascination with military uniforms, can be seen in one of the paintings completed between 1893 and 1895, *Artillerymen*, which is unique in his work. The careful placing of the artillery battery, as the soldiers stand around their gun against a landscape background, is one of Rousseau's most firmly constructed compositions. Such tiny details as the red facings and gold braid of the squadron sergeant-major's jacket are precisely delineated, while the painter clearly renders the psychological realism of the group's pride in their status.

Rousseau left the army as a private in 1868; he had applied for and been granted a discharge on his father's death in that year. The next year he married his first wife, Clémence Boitard, with whom he had seven children, only two of whom were to survive infancy. He entered the Paris Municipal Toll-collecting Service

(the Octroi) shortly afterward. Rousseau's duties were modest, although he enjoyed the status of being a minor public functionary, and the small pension that, unusually in this period, went with such a job was to be a vital factor in his

later decision to devote his life to painting.

In the toll-collecting service, Rousseau was employed in the surveillance of goods subject to excise duties brought into the city of Paris. This meant that he

spent a great deal of time in the suburbs, at the gates of the city, and along the banks of the Seine, all of which furnished subjects for his later paintings. Rousseau's weekly term of duty could be up to 70 hours, and although his work does not appear to have been onerous, these shift periods left him with very little time to paint. The growing family lived in modest circumstances, but Rousseau at least had the security of knowing that his post was pensionable and, as a public servant, his years spent in the infantry counted toward the reckonable service of his superannuation.

Despite, or perhaps because of, the mundane circumstances of his working life, Rousseau began to paint as a "Sunday artist" in his spare time from at least 1877, when his earliest work can be traced. The circumstances are not clear, but it appears that the understanding attitude of his employers after about 1885 allowed Rousseau to alter his shifts so that he could devote more time to his painting. His life as an artist, however, may be said to have truly begun only when he was almost 50, in 1893, when he felt enough confidence in the public recognition of his work to retire on his small pension.

Writing in the third person in his autobiographical notes of July 1895, *Portraits for the Coming Century*, Rousseau expressed with some feeling his lack of formal artistic training:

Since his [sic] parents were not well-to-do, he was compelled at first to follow another career, rather than the one to which his artistic disposition inclined him. It was not until 1885 that he began to work as an artist, after many disappointments, alone, with no teacher except nature and with occasional pieces of advice from Gérome and Clément.

As ever with Rousseau, it is extremely difficult to separate fact from fiction, although these autobiographical notes are a unique and invaluable source. The artists mentioned were well-known Salon painters, whose worldly success was admired by the aspiring young artist. Certainly it is true that Félix-Auguste Clément, who had worked himself up from modest beginnings, winning the prestigious, state-sponsored Prix de Rome, was Rousseau's neighbor for a time in the Rue de Sèvres. It seems possible that Clément offered both encouragement, and introductions to such prominent establishment painters as William-Adolphe Bouguereau and Jean-Léon Gérôme, to the young customs worker. The world of the academic artist was a highly competitive one, with a series of hurdles to be overcome and rewards to be won. Those rewards could be great, and public interest in contemporary art was unprecedented. Public exhibitions, particularly those at the Salon, attracted huge crowds and countless newspaper critiques.

Rousseau appears to have admired the highly finished academic style of history painters like Gérôme, who was famous for such scenes as *The Two Majesties* (*c*.1885), which depicts a splendid lion gazing at a blood-red sun across a desolate landscape. The painting can be seen as an influence on such Rousseau canvases as *The Sleeping Gypsy* (1897), with its expressive desert landscape and sharply delineated figures. From the middle of the century to around 1900, Salon painters such as Gérôme were noted for the high degree of symbolism in their often exotic subject-matter, and for the meticulous technique of their heroically-sized canvases.

These painters were known derogatively to their contemporaries as *Pompiers* (firemen), a reference to the helmets worn in history subjects, which bore a striking resemblance to contemporary firemen's headgear. *Pompier* paintings were exhibited among other contemporary works in the Luxembourg galleries (closed in 1939), for which Rousseau was to obtain a copyist's pass. This prestigious space was regarded as the first step toward the ultimate honor for the French artist of the nineteenth century, a place on the walls of the Louvre. This could only be achieved posthumously, ten years after the artist's death. Once won, artistic reputations, particularly among *Pompiers*, were jealously guarded. The Swiss painter, Félix Vallotton, is said to have commented, on first surveying the contemporary French art scene when he arrived in Paris in 1882: "*C'est plus facile d'être incendiaire que pompier*." (It is easier to be a firebug than a fireman.)

Although Rousseau omits to mention it in the autobiographical notes, it is likely that Clément or one of his circle wrote a reference for Rousseau to the Minister of Education, for by 1884, Rousseau had obtained a permit to copy works in the Louvre, the Luxembourg Museum and the Palace of Versailles. However, such forays into the ideal world of his "artistic disposition" were no substitute for the rigorous professional training

LEFT: Jean-Léon Gérôme, *Crossing the Desert*. Gérôme's desert landscapes influenced Rousseau's work in the 1890s.

BOTTOM: Rousseau, *The Sawmill; Outskirts of Paris*, c.1893-95 (oil on canvas, 10 × 19 inches, 25.5 × 45.5 cm. Photograph © 1995 The Art Institute of Chicago, IL, Bequest of Kate L. Brewster, 1950.133)

undergone by Rousseau's contemporaries, and it is true to say that like most so-called "naive" or "primitive" painters, Rousseau was essentially self-taught. This was one of several factors blocking his way when he tried to gain entry to official circles by submitting his paintings for exhibitions in the Salon, and he was refused, like most of his avant-garde contemporaries. These included Cézanne, who had dubbed the officially sponsored annual art exhibition "The Salon de Monsieur Bouguereau," so great was that artist's influence on the upholding of traditional standards.

Rousseau was in fact exceptional among artists working in Paris in this period in his lack of academic training. Cézanne himself, a mere five years Rousseau's junior, had studied at the Académie Suisse; Renoir, Monet and Whistler had undergone training under Charles Gleyre, and Van Gogh, Toulouse-Lautrec and Matisse were all students of Fernand Cormon, the academic painter whose public decorative schemes included murals for the Museum of Natural History in Paris.

Myself: Portrait-Landscape

However much he may have regretted his lack of formal training, Rousseau had no doubts concerning his own status as an artist. The clearest communication of his perceived self-image is the self-portrait, *Myself, Portrait Landscape* (1895), which was exhibited at the Salon des Indépendants a mere two years after the painter had retired from the toll service to work as a full-time artist. In the same year, Rousseau provided his notes for the unpublished *Portraits for the Coming Century*. After the account of the deprivations of his artistic beginnings quoted above, Rousseau concludes (in the third person): "He continued to improve his mastery of the original genre he had developed and is now on the way to becoming one of our best realist painters."

Rousseau appears to have regarded the combination of landscape and portrait as one of his specialities and it may be this that he refers to as "the original genre he had developed." The precise nature of Rousseau's self-styled realism is impossible to quantify, but the ambitions of the 46-year old painter are presented in this self-portrait with a startling clarity.

He presents himself full-length, a format usually reserved for persons of importance and seldom adopted at the time for self-portraits. He represents himself as he wished to appear to posterity, a dignified, commanding figure, with a full beard and floppy beret (like those worn by Rembrandt in his later self-portraits) signifying his artistic status. He is dressed entirely in black, a color defined as a powerful symbol of modernity by the poet and critic Charles Baudelaire, in the famous essay *On the Heroism of Modern Life* in his review of the Salon of 1846. Baudelaire had suggested that:

Great colorists know how to create color with a black coat, a white cravat and a gray background . . . The life of our city [Paris] is rich in poetic and marvelous subjects. We are enveloped and steeped as though in an atmosphere of the marvelous; but we do not notice it.

Baudelaire's words have particular relevance to Rousseau's work. Rousseau's resonant use of black, as seen in this painting, was much admired by his contemporaries, and his work is indeed "rich in poetic and marvelous subjects," whether the wonders of modern Paris, with himself at the center of them as here, or the extraordinary fantasies of the jungle subjects of his imagination.

In *Myself, Portrait-Landscape*, Rousseau holds his palette and brush like badges of office of the artist's life to which he aspires. He stands on the quays of the Seine, where he had worked until two years before, wearing the very different badge of his service in this capacity – a saber at his belt in case of trouble with smugglers. Behind Rousseau, and dwarfed by his giant figure, is a boat flying the maritime flags of all nations, some of them imaginary emblems, some real, such as the Tricolor and the Union Jack. The relative size and position of the boat and quayside to the central figure would

Gabillaud's *Souvenir of the Universal Exposition in 1889* pays homage to Gustave Eiffel and his magnificent tower.

d'Orsay, one of a pair commemorating the relief of the Siege of Paris in 1870, in which such balloons played a major part.

Rousseau's giant figure is shown as larger than the most significant symbol of French modernity, the Eiffel Tower, built for the 1889 World's Fair, and for Rousseau, unusually among artists at the time, a potent symbol of technological progress. The World's Fair itself was also an object of fascination; he even wrote a three-act vaudeville play on the subject, which he tried to sell, to no avail, to the Châtelet Theatre. The Eiffel Tower came to symbolize Paris itself in the work of a younger generation of artists, such as Marc Chagall and Robert Delaunay. Robert and Sonia Delaunay were among Rousseau's early admirers, and in his key work of 1910-12, *The City of Paris*, Robert Delaunay incorporates a homage to Rousseau in the form of a "quotation" from this painting by placing the prow of the boat and its festoon of flags in a prominent place in the composition.

That Rousseau regarded *Myself, Portrait-Landscape* as a key painting of iconic status can be deduced from his later additions, which can be read as the equivalent of a writer bringing his autobiography up to date in subsequent editions. On the palette are inscribed the names of his first wife, Clémence, and his second wife Jacqueline, whom he was not to marry until 1899. Another later amendment is the addition in his buttonhole of the badge of the *"palmes académiques"* he was awarded in 1904.

The Salon des Indépendants
In the book of press cuttings he kept so meticulously all his life, Rousseau writes regretfully of the fate of the two paintings (both now lost) he submitted to the Salon of 1885: "one was slashed with a penknife, and then they cheated me out of payment." There is no record of this incident other than Rousseau's own, but it is certainly true that by the time that Rousseau was thinking of exhibiting his paintings where they would receive the maximum attention, the Salon was beginning to lose its prestigious position. Official sponsorship was withdrawn in 1881, and various independent groups of artists in Paris began to set up their own exhibitions.

The most important of these was the Salon of Independent Artists, *le Salon des Indépendants*, which was founded in 1884 by Seurat, Signac and others to stand in opposition to the official Salon.

appear to symbolize Rousseau's literal "putting behind him" of nearly 20 years as a minor public functionary.

In making himself so prominent in *Myself, Portrait-Landscape*, Rousseau reverts to the convention that had reigned before the Renaissance method of mathematically founded linear perspective gained currency in Europe. In the earlier convention the most important figure in a painting, the Madonna for example, dominated the picture space. Rousseau would have seen the work of such early Flemish painters as Hans Memling on his study visits to the Louvre. Memling's

work employs these earlier conventions of proportion, and his bright color and meticulous technique of painting in oils would surely have attracted Rousseau's attention.

In his self-portrait, Rousseau's head is on a level with a modern marvel, the hot air balloon. Later paintings contain ample evidence of Rousseau's fascination with the conquest of the air by modern machines, such as the balloon and the airplane. Use of such a motif as the balloon is highly unusual at the time, and Rousseau may have had in mind a painting by Puvis de Chavannes, now in the Musée

Paul Gauguin, *Nave Nave Fenua (Delightful Land)*, Guerin 28, *c.*1893-95 (woodcut, 14 × 8 inches, 35.4 × 20.1 cm. Photograph © 1994 The Art Institute of Chicago, IL, Clarence Buckingham Collection, 1938.261 recto)

The Salon des Indépendants was of major importance up until the beginning of World War I. Its annual exhibitions became the main arena for the showing of Post-Impressionist art, and such artists as Vincent van Gogh, Paul Gauguin and Henri de Toulouse-Lautrec were regular exhibitors from its first years. There was no selection committee at the Indépendants, and any artist could exhibit on payment of a modest fee.

It was providential for Rousseau that such an arena was offered in the years in which he was thinking of giving up his everyday work and devoting his life to painting, as otherwise his work would never have received notice in a public exhibition. In August 1886, at the first major exhibition of 500 paintings at the Indépendants, Rousseau seized his chance and, at the age of 42, hung *A Carnival Evening* and three other paintings, whose identity has been disputed and are probably now lost, like so much of Rousseau's work.

A Carnival Evening is remarkably assured in design and execution for a beginner, and it seems likely that Rousseau had been painting for several years before he took the decisive step to exhibit. The motif of a figure or figures in the clearing of a wood or forest is used in other early paintings, but nowhere with as much conviction as in this winter landscape. The stark moonlit scene is reminiscent of the work of the German Romantic painter, Caspar David Friedrich, but the figures may have been taken from a popular print or even an advertisement. The male figure is costumed as a Pierrot and may owe something to the paintings of Watteau that Rousseau would have seen in the Louvre.

The mood of the painting is dreamlike, and both the technical expertise and the delicacy of the colors were admired by no less an artist than Camille Pissarro, who commented on the "rightness of its values, the richness of its tints," when it was exhibited at the Salon des Indépendants in 1886. Today we may wonder at the exactness of Rousseau's design and the dreamlike lyricism of the scene. The moon and the massing of the clouds gives the painting a haunting quality, as if it were a stage set, and this theatrical atmosphere may have seemed particularly appropriate to the carnival season of winter.

This shrewd launching of Rousseau's public career attracted immediate notice, and brought him into the orbit of the most exciting and innovative painters of his day. The popular press, however, was less kind. The journal *Le Soleil* held the painting up to ridicule, describing it to its readers as:

A negro and negress in costume, are lost in a zinc forest . . . beneath a circular moon that shines but does not illuminate anything, while under the black sky a highly bizarre constellation, made up of a blue cone and a pink cone, is affixed.

Despite such criticism, and encouraged by the interest taken in his work, Rousseau hung three paintings and five drawings at the Salon des Indépendants the following year. He continued to exhibit on average five paintings a year to the end of his life, except for the years of his most prolific work, 1891, 1895, 1896 and 1902, when he exhibited twice that number.

In 1891, the year in which the Indépendants held a retrospective exhibit of the work of Van Gogh, Rousseau submitted

Eugène Delacroix, *Encounter Between a Lion and a Tiger* (National Gallery, Prague) prefigures Rousseau's interest in similar jungle scenes.

his first jungle scenes. One of these was *Tropical Storm with a Tiger (Surprise!)*, now in the National Gallery, London. The young Swiss artist Félix Vallotton, who reviewed the exhibition for *Le Journal Suisse* gives a telling account of Rousseau's work and its reception:

In spite of those doubled up with stifled laughter ... Rousseau becomes more and more astonishing each year, but he commands attention and, in any event, is earning a nice little reputation ... he is a terrible neighbor, since he crushes everything else. His tiger surprising its prey ought not to be missed: it is the alpha and omega of painting.

Rousseau himself was well aware of all that he owed the Indépendants, and in 1906 painted *Liberty inviting Artists to take part in the Twenty-second Exhibition of the Salon des Indépendants*, now in Tokyo. His tribute to the Indépendants is an intriguing mixture of factual detail, drawn from his personal experience of the institution, and allegorical fantasy. The long lines of artists, among whom can be discerned several women, converge symmetrically toward the open entrance of the Salon, with their paintings either under their arms or stacked in handcarts (as Rousseau brought his own work for exhibition). To the left of the picture, yet more paintings are arriving in small horse-drawn waggons.

The vividly realized allegorical elements include the figure of Liberty in the sky, and the lion (who here, as so often in Rousseau's work, represents independence and courage), which rests its paws on a scroll of artists of the Société, Rousseau's own name clearly visible. These allegorical elements co-exist with the everyday in the same space. This is particularly marked in the positioning of the two most prominently placed figures in the foreground, who may represent Rousseau himself and Paul Signac, who was exceptionally tall. The whole scene is made even more celebratory by the flags and pennants, which, as in *Myself, Portrait-Landscape*, are partly real – the two huge banners in the colors of the City of Paris and of France, and the smaller tricolor and Stars and Stripes – and partly imaginary.

In 1911, the year after his death, the Salon paid tribute to Rousseau with a posthumous exhibition of his work at the XXVIIth Salon des Indépendants. An entire room was devoted to his work, which did much to cement Rousseau's lasting fame.

The Rousseau Legend
In the last years of his life, Rousseau's circle of admirers included most of the avant-garde artists and critics of his time. Apart from the distinctive qualities of his work, it would seem that Picasso and his contemporaries also admired Rousseau's absolute dedication to his calling as a painter, despite the extreme privations of

Guillaume Apollinaire in about 1907.

his life. Separated from his fellow artists by his lack of formal artistic training and by social class, Rousseau was to suffer extreme poverty, but was in no doubt of his own place in history. At the Banquet given in his honor in Picasso's studio in the Bateau Lavoir in Montmartre, in November 1908, Rousseau offered Picasso and the assembled company a famous assessment of his self-perceived status: "We are the greatest painters of our time, you in the Egyptian manner, I in the Modern."

Guillaume Apollinaire was in his early twenties when he first met Rousseau, who was by then in his sixties and attracting considerable notice at the Indépendants and elsewhere. In the early years of the century Apollinaire was fast becoming an active champion of most of the modern movements in art, from Cubism to Surrealism, which were to make Paris the center of aesthetic activity until World War II. Apollinaire was among the first to recognize the unique talents of Picasso, and with others of the younger generation, such as the radical playwright Alfred Jarry and the painters and designers Robert and Sonia Delaunay, he honored Rousseau in his lifetime and helped spread his reputation throughout Europe and America after the painter's death.

It is to Apollinaire, whose portrait with Marie Laurençin Rousseau was to paint as *The Muse Inspiring the Poet*, that we owe many of the legends surrounding Rousseau, legends that are so potent that they are difficult to dislodge from the popular view of his work. Rousseau's unrivaled jungle paintings, the earliest of which is probably *Tropical Storm with a Tiger (Surprise!)* of 1891, for example, owe everything to the power of his extraordinary imagination and his visits to the tropical greenhouses of the Jardins des Plantes in Paris, and nothing whatsoever to the mythical period of military service in Mexico as a regimental musician, related as fact by Apollinaire.

The fact remains, however, that Rousseau's work was admired by many of the leading avant-garde artists of the time and his seminal place in the history of art was ensured in his own lifetime. Perhaps most significant of all is the regard in which he was held by Picasso, who appears to have known Rousseau from the time he first settled in Paris in 1904. Picasso purchased several of Rousseau's paintings, with which he was often photographed in later years and which

now hang in the Musée Picasso, Paris. The *Portrait of a Woman* (c.1895) which he bought for 5 francs from a secondhand dealer and hung as the focus of the famous 1908 banquet in honor of Rousseau, Picasso was to describe as "a work of French insight, of decision and clearness . . . one of the most revealing French psychological portraits."

Picasso's view of Rousseau was radically different from Apollinaire's, close friend though the writer was at the time. Picasso admired Rousseau as a fellow painter, and his own work both during the Cubist years and later, can be seen to have been influenced by Rousseau. This influence was communicated not only through the works owned by Picasso

himself, but through the paintings he must have seen in Rousseau's studio and at the important group exhibitions at which Rousseau was regularly showing his work. These included the Salon des Indépendants and the Salon d'Automne, as well as the collection of the famous dealer and champion of avant-garde art, Ambroise Vollard, who had held the first one-man exhibitions of Picasso's own work in 1901, and of Matisse's work in 1904.

Rousseau's place in the history of art may be assured, but the precise nature of that place is contradictory and impossible to categorize. His finest work was produced at the turn of the twentieth century and he continued to exhibit all

The Jardin des Plantes in Paris, *c*.1900.
Rousseau's visits there informed his jungle
paintings.

his life at the Salon des Indépendants alongside such contemporaries as Cézanne, Seurat, Van Gogh and other leading Post-Impressionists. However his association with the younger generation of artists is no less remarkable. At the Salon d'Automne of 1905, Rousseau exhibited *The Hungry Lion* in the same room as paintings by Matisse, Derain, Vlaminck, and other painters for whom color was the primary means of expression. The critics were incensed to such a degree by the paintings that (perhaps inspired in part by Rousseau's painting) they christened the room "the cage of the wild beasts," or the "*cage aux fauves*," which gave the painters of the first of the modern movements in art, the Fauves, their name.

Rousseau's supreme confidence in his own work was matched by a shrewd sense of how best to bring it to public notice. Despite Guillaume Apollinaire's and Alfred Jarry's later assertions, no-one discovered Rousseau, and what might be termed the Rousseau Legend, which began in the artist's lifetime, has to be re-

garded with some scepticism. Nonetheless, Apollinaire's most famous story in *Il y a* of Rousseau at work has a certain ring of truth about it:

Rousseau had so strong a sense of reality that when he painted one of his fantastic subjects, he was sometimes so frightened that, trembling all over, he had to open the window.

Apollinaire goes on to relate that Rousseau was much calmer while painting portraits.

I posed a number of times for the Douanier, and before anything else he carefully measured my nose, my mouth, my ears, my forehead, my hands, my entire body, and he then inscribed on the canvas the measurements reduced in proper proportion. During all this, since posing is extremely boring, the Douanier sang songs of his youth and of the time he had spent in the toll service.

This account must refer to the year before Rousseau's death, when he portrayed Apollinaire and the artist Marie Laurençin in a double "portrait-landscape" as a visual token of friendship

known as *The Muse Inspiring the Poet* (1907), which exists in two versions. Marie Laurençin had met Apollinaire only months before, although their association was to last for many years. She is represented as an allegorical figure in loose classical robes, her head garlanded with Rousseau's favorite flowers, pansies. One of her hands is raised in what appears to be a gesture of blessing, reminiscent of figures in Renaissance religious paintings, and the other rests protectively on the poet's shoulders. Marie Laurençin did not attend sittings regularly; indeed by December 1908, Rousseau was complaining, "I am still awaiting the charming Muse to pose for me at least once."

When the portrait was finally completed, either Laurençin or Apollinaire (or possibly both) complained that the famously svelte and elegant Laurençin had been made to appear fat. To this Rousseau is said to have replied that, as Guillaume was a great poet, he needed a large muse. Be that as it may, Apollinaire did not pay for the portrait, despite several tactful requests from the luckless

14

BELOW: The playwright Alfred Jarry pictured in about 1898; he claimed responsibility for "discovering" Rousseau.

BOTTOM: Marie Laurençin's painting of Apollinaire, Picasso, herself and their circle (Musée National d'Art Moderne, Paris)

Rousseau, who wrote to Apollinaire with a final plea after the painting had been hung in the Salon des Indépendants in April, 1909: "It upsets me to have to write this to you . . . I hope that you will be good enough to send me a little money by return."

Alfred Jarry and Folk Imagery

However vivid Apollinaire's stories, it is to Rousseau's other literary admirer, the poet, critic and avant-garde playwright, Alfred Jarry (1873-1907), that we owe the famous myth of the "discovery" of Rousseau. Jarry, like Rousseau, was born in Laval. He was the creator of the extraordinary *Ubu* plays, which caused such a sensation when *Ubu Roi* was first performed in December 1896. Jarry was fond of relating one of many practical jokes he played on the gullible and good-natured Rousseau. Writing of his "discovery" of the painter, Jarry said he confronted Rousseau at his customs post on the loading quays of the Seine, earnestly informing him, "I can see in your face that you are a painter. You must become one." Jarry then relates that he "directed" Rousseau's first painting.

Rousseau, *La Guerre (The War)*, c.1895
(lithograph on orange paper, © 1995 Board of
Trustees, National Gallery of Art, Washington,
D.C., Rosenwald Collection)

Although this story is almost certainly apocryphal, the remarkably precocious Jarry, who at 21 was almost 30 years Rousseau's junior, was certainly profoundly affected by Rousseau's paintings at the Indépendants and, when he later became one of Rousseau's many friends, by his generosity and open-heartedness. Like Apollinaire, Jarry was to receive Rousseau's ultimate gift of friendship – a portrait of himself, with his pet chameleon. This is long since lost, but Jarry was to record that, after the scandalous opening performance of *Ubu Roi* in December 1896 left him penniless, he lived for some time in Rousseau's studio, although the painter could ill afford such hospitality.

Jarry was so impressed by what he saw of Rousseau's work and ideas (ideas that in many ways were close to his own) that he persuaded Rémy de Gourmont, the publisher of the journal *L'Ymagier*, to publish Rousseau's only lithograph, *War*, in January 1895. Jarry had helped found *L'Ymagier* to provide original graphic works based on the traditions of folk art. The first issue of the journal contained the following explanation of its aims:

Running alongside and underlying printed literature runs the stream of oral tradition, tales, legends and folk songs. There is folk imagery, too, today represented in the products of the Epinal workshop . . . In the form of leaflets or pamphlets, that ephemeral imagery is known only to archeologists or a few lovers of art: it is our starting point here, and the rest of the contents of *L'Ymagier*, are but extras . . . or objects for study and comparison.

L'Ymagier published other elements of what would now be called folk art, old songs and poems from the vernacular tradition, elements that Jarry was at this time trying to incorporate and bring up to date in the verbal imagery of the *Ubu* plays.

Rousseau had long used such elements in his work. His painting *A Hundred Years of Independence* (1892), which is itself based on a popular woodcut, carried the inscription "The people dance around the two Republics, that of 1792 and that of 1892, holding hands, to the tune of *Auprès de ma blonde qu'il fait bon fait bon dormir.*"

In 1894 Rousseau exhibited *War*, his largest and most ambitious canvas to date. Jarry was yet to make Rousseau's acquaintance, but *War* must have seemed like the realization of Jarry's dream of a modern "Ymagist" who would revive folk images and make them part of the modern mainstream. Rousseau had worked on *War* during the winter of 1893-94, in the year of his retirement from the customs service, and as he must have expected, it attracted huge attention at the Salon des Indépendants.

In this powerful and alarming painting, which is quite unlike anything else that survives of Rousseau's work, the painter's imagination was certainly fired by such popular exotic imagery as the brightly colored Epinal chromolithograph *Bataille des Pyramides*. Rousseau appended an inscription, "War (terrifying, she passes by, leaving behind on all sides despair, tears and ruin.)" War is personified as what appears to be a ferocious child, riding through a nightmarish ravaged landscape. Jarry described the painting in his review of the exhibition in the following evocative terms:

16

RIGHT: The Epinal chromolithograph *Bataille des Pyramides*, which influenced Rousseau's harrowing picture of *War* (1894).

BELOW: Rousseau with his violin, pictured in his studio *c.*1906, with *The Country Wedding*, painted the previous year, behind him.

With legs outstretched, the horrorstruck steed stretches its neck with its dancer's head, black leaves inhabit the mauve clouds, and fragments of débris fall like pine cones among the axolotls attacked by the bright-beaked crows.

For once in Rousseau's work we can trace at least some of the sources for the painting. The Epinal print has already been noted, and to this might be added a newspaper caricature, *The Tsar*, depicting a cloaked figure astride a horse, who rides over a heap of bodies in a manner comparable to Rousseau's creature. Following the horseman is a flurry of crows. Whatever the contemporary sources, Rousseau has created a terrifying image of the destruction of war, one fit to rank with Pieter Brueghel's *Triumph of Death*.

Rousseau's treatment of the ravaged landscape (very different from his usual burgeoning greenery) and his use of symbolic color, may be compared with *We are Making a New World* (1917) by Paul Nash, who worked as an Official War Artist on the Western Front, and created a powerful expression of "the bitter truth" of World War I.

The Full-Time Painter

In 1893, Rousseau retired on his small pension of 1010 francs per quarter, living in poverty-stricken circumstances and augmenting the tiny income he received from his painting with occasional violin lessons. For many years Rousseau tried to find additional sources of income. He entered various painting competitions without success, and worked as an inspector of sales and distribution for a local Paris newspaper, *Le Petit Parisien*. He even wrote a play for the Châtelet Theater, *The Revenge of a Russian Orphan*, which was not accepted and was published only in 1947, by the Swiss Surrealist poet Tristan Tzara.

In 1899 Rousseau married for a second time. His wife was a widow, Joséphine Noury, and until her death in 1904 she tried without success to sell her husband's paintings from the small stationery shop she ran. Only two of Rousseau's seven children survived infancy. His surviving son, who shared a room with the painter after he was widowed for the second time, was 18 when he died.

Rousseau painted small pendant portraits of himself and Joséphine in the first years of their marriage. A year after Rousseau's death, his first biographer, Wilhelm Uhde, wrote of the two figures:

Neither of them is young. Without any decoration or symbol the heads stand out against the background, but a lamp, unobtrusively set next to them, suggests calm domesticity and happiness far more evocatively than a home painted in all its details could have done.

A contemporary view of the 1900 Exposition
Générale in Paris.

The portraits were to have a distinguished ownership. Originally in Robert Delaunay's collection and selected among other Rousseaus for reproduction in the *Blaue Reiter* almanac, they were bought by Picasso, and can be seen in photographs of the artist at work in his studio. They now hang in the Musée Picasso, Paris. Joséphine is probably also depicted in the double portrait of *c*.1890-1899, *The Present and the Past*. This is much more elaborate in both form and content than the pendant portraits, and to it Rousseau appended one of his own poems as an inscription:

Separated one from the other
[And] from those they had loved,
Both remarried,
Yet remained faithful in spirit.

In 1902, Rousseau was appointed one of 600 teachers in a new adult education scheme in Paris, the Philotechnic Association, which provided Sunday morning lessons. In the following year he began giving lessons in "Elocution, Music, Painting and Singing" in his own studio,

for adults and children. The sums charged for such private tuition were very modest and did little to alleviate the straitened circumstances in which Rousseau was to live for the rest of his life. Indeed, in the first years of the century Rousseau was unable to pay for the essential materials of his work. He had run up a debt of 614 francs to his supplier of paints and canvases on credit, and was taken to court in December, 1904, and ordered to pay off his debt at 10 francs a month.

Despite Rousseau's poverty, he was generous to a fault, and was well enough thought of in the neighborhood in which he lived, the Plaisance quarter, south of the *gare* Montparnasse, to be commissioned to paint portraits of local tradesmen's children, although he asked very little for his painstaking labor and may even have been paid in kind. It seems likely that Rousseau painted some of his child portraits of this period as a way of thanking his neighbors for their kindness to him. He was godfather to various neighbors' children; he painted the portrait *Girl in Pink* in 1907, three years

before his death, for the family of Charlotte Papouin, to whose younger sister he was godfather. Blocks of stone at Charlotte's feet almost certainly refer to her father's trade of stonemason. The portrait is reminiscent of American nineteenth-century folk art in its rigid frontality, and in the attention given to the dress the child is wearing.

The most elaborate of these portraits of neighboring families is the splendid group portrait, *Père Juniet's Cart* (1908). Claude and Anna Juniet ran a grocer's shop on the intersection of the rue Perrel, where Rousseau lived, and the rue Vercingétorix, and the photographs from which Rousseau painted the family survive, showing Rousseau himself seated next to Claude Juniet (who also trained horses), the white mare Rosa, in whom Père Junier took particular pride, and the three family dogs.

Even before his retirement from the customs service, Rousseau's paintings had begun to receive official recognition at the Salon des Indépendants. He collected all his reviews, however unfavor-

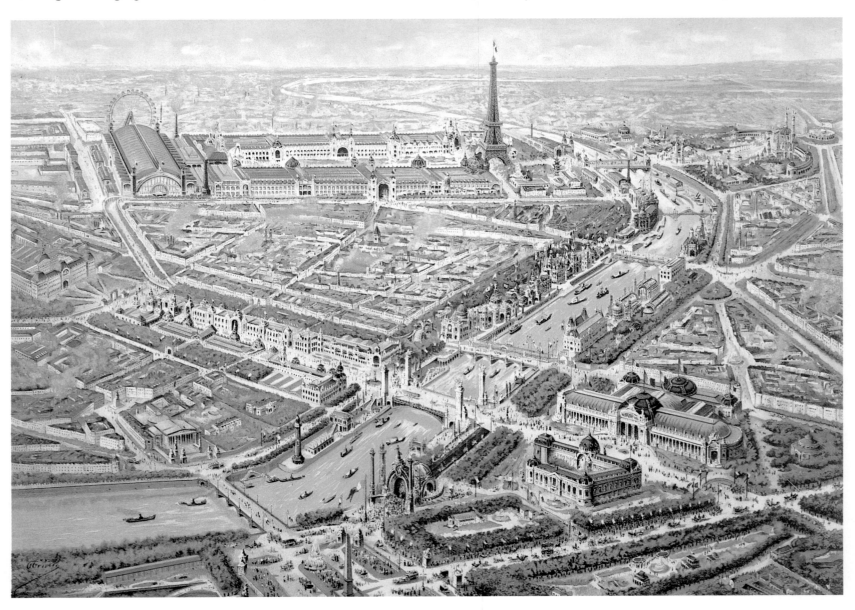

BELOW: Rousseau's studio reconstructed today.

BOTTOM: The title page of Rousseau's *Clémence* waltz, named for his first wife and published in 1904.

able, and pasted them painstakingly in his notebooks. At first (in the late 1880s) the reviewers were intrigued by Rousseau's "primitive," "sincere" and "curious" images. From 1894 onward, however, Rousseau became the target of prolonged and bitter attacks as an "annual aberration" for "the scoffing public," and some members of the Indépendants were prepared to drop him. It appears that on this occasion Henri de Toulouse-Lautrec defended Rousseau, who gratefully continued to exhibit with the group for the rest of his life.

From this period on, Rousseau was never without staunch and powerful defenders of this caliber. Camille Pissarro, who, together with Gauguin, particularly admired Rousseau's use of black, was prepared to recognize that in the power of Rousseau's images "emotion takes the place of training." Rousseau sent a pen-and-ink self-portrait as an illustration to his written statement of autobiography in 1895. He had heard on the grapevine that there was to be a publication on leading artists of the day, entitled *Portraits for the Coming Century*, and he submitted his autobiography as though it had been written by someone else. Although in fact never published, the notes provide not only a revealing analysis of Rousseau's own view of his vocation as an artist but also, by their omissions, a telling account of the way in which the artist regarded the 49 years of his life before he became a painter. These years

of work, marriage and family life are dismissed in a sentence, as Rousseau explains that he "was first forced, owing to his parents' lack of fortune, to pursue a career different from that to which his artistic tastes called him . . . It is only after great hardships that he succeeded in making a name for himself among some of the artists of the day."

Rousseau describes himself as painted in *Myself, Portrait-Landscape* and as he

appeared in the accompanying pen-and-ink sketch. The beard was to be shaved off in later years, perhaps on the occasion of his second marriage in 1899, as it does not appear in his self-portrait of that period, painted shortly after his marriage to Joséphine.

His appearance is notable because of his bushy beard, and he has long been a member of the Indépendants, believing as he does that complete freedom of production must be allowed to any innovator whose thought aspires toward the beautiful and the good. He will never forget those members of the Press who have been able to understand him and support him in his moments of discouragement and who assisted him in achieving his goals.

It is difficult to believe that the shrewd, if childishly generous, painter was not writing without irony here.

The Banquet Years

Despite such revealing fragments of autobiographical writing, it is not until after the death of Rousseau's second wife Joséphine in 1903, leaving him just seven years to live, that we are able to bring the painter into sharper focus and to learn more about his way of life in the petit-bourgeois district of Plaisance, where he lived in a single room which also served as a studio. He accepted the lack of space with his usual grace, explaining to his friends that it meant that when he woke

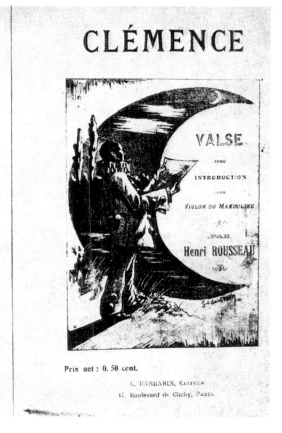

HENRI ROUSSEAU

Picasso in about 1908, in his studio in the
Bateau-Lavoir.

labored long and hard over such
elaborate canvases. He was dependent on
his pension of 1010 francs a quarter and
was never able to pay off his debts for
essential art supplies, but he was proud of
the relatively small sums he earned for his
work. He noted them methodically in the
accounts he kept in a book intended for
laundry lists: "Sold to Monsieur Delaunay, a lovely Mexican landscape, with
monkeys, for 100 francs ... Sold to
Madame la Baronne d'Oettingen, my self
portrait for 300 francs."

Rousseau's forays into the world of
Parisian high society were a marked
feature of his last years. Robert and Sonia
Delaunay introduced him into the circle
of Delaunay's mother, who had traveled

widely and told tales of exotic climes to
visitors to her fashionable salon in what is
now the Avenue George V. In contemporary photographs of her salon,
Madame Delaunay appears to be sur-
rounded by huge palms and other
tropical plants, like those in the palm
houses of the Botanic Gardens with
which Rousseau was so familiar. Accord-
ing to Sonia Delaunay, Rousseau's visits
to Madame Delaunay's salon provided
the impetus for *The Snake Charmer*,
commissioned by Madame Delaunay in
1907. Robert and Sonia Delaunay in-
herited the painting after Madame
Delaunay's death and, when forced to
sell it in 1922, Robert ensured in a com-
plex legal maneuver that it would, in due

course, be hung as part of the national
collection in the Louvre, the ultimate
accolade for a modern French painter.

By happy chance *The Snake Charmer*,
together with *War*, is now in the Musée
d'Orsay, where instructive comparisons
and contrasts may be made, as the two
paintings (which are polar opposites in
Rousseau's work, demonstrating his
extraordinary range) hang alongside
works by Rousseau's contemporaries at
the Salon des Indépendants, Georges
Seurat and Paul Signac. In the context of
such theoretically based works as
Seurat's *The Circus*, it is particularly revealing to recall Delaunay's words on
Rousseau's work: "He had no theories at
all . . . for him the picture was a primal
surface with which he had to deal physi-
cally in order to project his thought."

Delaunay's painterly admiration for
Rousseau's work can be clearly seen in his
own best known canvas, *The City of Paris*
(1910-1912). Along with the Three
Graces, symbolizing the traditional
beauty of historic Paris, and the Eiffel
Tower, representing the modernity of
the city, this contains a direct quotation
from Rousseau's *Myself, Portrait-Landscape* in the form of the boat in the background decked out in flags.

Soirées Familiales et Artistiques

Some time in 1907, at Madame Delaunay's salon, Rousseau met the young
American painter Max Weber, who was
studying painting in Paris and, by the
time he met Rousseau, training in
Matisse's studio. Weber was an enthu-
siastic advocate of Rousseau's work from
his first meeting with the painter. He
showed the canvases he could afford to
buy from the artist, and some drawings
Rousseau had given him, in the first one-
man exhibition of Rousseau's work out-
side France, at the Alfred Stieglitz gallery
in New York in 1910.

By this time Rousseau had begun to
hold his famous Saturday evening
parties, the *soirées familiales et artistiques*
which are so potent a part of the Rousseau legend. Max Weber's recollections
of meeting Rousseau at Madame Delaunay's salon provide a vivid image of the
painter in his last years:

A round-shouldered genial old man, small of
stature with a smiling face and bright eyes,
carrying a cane, entered the room. He was
warmly received and one could see that he
was pleased to find himself among so many
friends and admirers.

Rousseau in his studio, *c*.1908.

When Weber left Paris in December 1908, Rousseau gave a special *soirée* "in honor of the farewell to Monsieur Weber." The *soirées* were often given on much slimmer pretexts, and Rousseau organized these parties in the modest circumstances of his studio in the rue Perrel with extraordinary meticulousness. He issued invitations printed in different colors, with the formal part of the evening laid out like a concert program. The list invariably contained, among the recitations and orchestral pieces, "Monsieur Rousseau (violin solo) with his works and creations," while Rousseau's music, painting and elocution lessons were usefully publicized on the back.

The guest list and performers formed an extraordinarily eclectic mixture. Rousseau's child pupils and adult students were invited to perform to neighbors and local tradespeople, who were joined by a significant majority of the most exciting and innovatory artists and writers of the time. Rousseau was now in his mid-60s and most of the

avant-garde visitors were a generation younger. Some were invited to perform – Max Weber, who had a fine tenor voice, sang and Georges Braque played his accordion.

The list of guests at these gatherings is indeed a starry one, including as it does Picasso, his mistress Fernande Olivier, Max Jacob, Apollinaire, Marie Laurençin and Constantin Brancusi among many others. Max Weber's account of his first visit to Rousseau's studio does something to explain the extraordinary attraction the painter had for a younger generation:

I shall never forget (it) as long as I live, I felt I had been favored by the gods to meet one of the most inspiring and precious personalities of all Paris . . . "Here," I say to myself, "is a man, an artist, a poet whose friendship and advice I must cultivate and cherish" . . . By a sacred sense of privacy he was shielded from the snobbery, pretense, and sophistication which was rife in the art circles of the time . . . there is nothing chameleon about him.

Apotheosis
In 1908 came the most famous banquet of all, organized not by Rousseau, for his friends and Plaisance neighbors, but by Picasso at his studio up the steep slopes of Montmartre in the Bateau Lavoir, with Rousseau as guest of honor. The banquet is the richest and most resonant occasion in the Rousseau legend, although the event was real enough. The eyewitness accounts agree on certain key points, through the haze of alcohol and goodwill, such as Rousseau's evident delight at this tribute to him. He was so charmed that he retained his place of honor on the impromptu dais, made out of a chair placed on a packing crate, while wax dripped on to his head from the candles in the Chinese lanterns festooning the studio.

Rousseau's *Portrait of a Woman*, which Picasso had recently purchased, hung garlanded and inscribed "Honneur à Rousseau," in the place of honor. The guests included Fernande Olivier, who was then living with Picasso, Georges Braque, Max Jacob, Marie Laurençin,

BELOW: The exterior of Rousseau's studio.

RIGHT: Rousseau in his studio, shortly before his death in 1910, pictured with *Forest Landscape with Setting Sun*.

and Gertrude and Leo Stein. They waited and waited for the food and wine which had been ordered from the grocery chain, Félix Potin (which still trades today). Unfortunately the order had been placed by Picasso for the following day. The food and wine which eventually appeared included, it would seem from the various accounts of the occasion, some 50 bottles of wine and a surprisingly large quantity of tins of sardines. It was procured from neighboring shops to make an impromptu feast much enjoyed by the assembled company.

Rousseau played his waltz *Clémence*, and made the famous declaration to his host, "We two are the greatest painters of our time, you in the Egyptian style, I in the Modern." The evening was full of such memorable quotations, not the least of which was Apollinaire's moving and apparently impromptu tribute to his friend, which included the following lines:

> You remember, Rousseau, the Aztec landscape
> The forests where the mango and pineapple grew,
> The monkeys sucking out the juice of watermelons,
> And the blond emperor they shot down there,
> The pictures you paint, you saw out in Mexico . . .
> Valiant soldier, you swapped your tunic For the customs officer's blue jacket.

Maurice Raynal, who attended the banquet, recorded that Apollinaire's tribute also included the following toast:

> We are gathered to celebrate your fame,
> And so let us drink the wine Picasso is pouring
> To honor you, for it is time to drink it Crying all in chorus, "Long live! Long live Rousseau!"

Despite such tributes from his peers, Rousseau was beset by poverty to the very end of his life. A few months before the banquet, Rousseau had been imprisoned for a month at La Santé prison, before standing trial for embezzlement and forgery in 1909, duped by one of his former pupils, an employee of the Bank of France, who took full responsibility for the offence at the trial. Rousseau was given a suspended sentence, after one of his tropical paintings with monkeys had been produced as evidence of his guilelessness. His defence lawyer pleaded:

This morning [Rousseau] said to me : "If I am condemned, it will not be an injustice for me, it will be a misfortune for art." Well now, members of the jury, give Rousseau back to art; spare this exceptional creature. You do not have the right to condemn a primitive.

Rousseau continued to work hard on his paintings, including the double portrait of Apollinaire and Marie Laurencin, *The Muse Inspiring the Poet*. He wrote frequent sad letters to Apollinaire about his lack of means, regretting the fact that he had to ask to be paid for the painting,

But I have had too many reverses to do otherwise. I have my pension, true enough: how could I do without it? But I have not been able to save anything, unfortunately, and when painting a picture which requires two or three months work, I must live somehow and furnish my own materials.

Yet still he continued to paint, producing some of his finest works, including several superb tropical landscapes and *The Dream*, his largest canvas. He submitted this to the Indépendants in March 1910, writing to Apollinaire: "I have submitted my large picture; everyone likes it. I hope you will deploy your literary gifts and avenge me for all the insults and setbacks I have received." Apollinaire devoted a lengthy review to the painting in *L'Intransigéant* of 18 March 1910, concluding, "In this painting we find beauty that is indisputable . . . I don't believe anyone will dare laugh this year . . . Ask the painters: they are unanimous – they admire."

Four months before he died, Rousseau wrote to a critic of his work:

I cannot now change my style, which I acquired, as you can imagine, by dint of stubborn labor . . . if I have kept my naiveté, it is because Monsieur Gérome . . . as well as Monsieur Clément . . . always told me to keep it; in the future you won't find it shocking any longer.

Rousseau's supreme self-confidence is linked here with his consciousness of the conceptual nature of his own work. This is seen most clearly in the tropical landscapes, such as *The Dream*. Writing to the critic André Dupont, Rousseau explained his concept in the following manner:

I am writing in response to your friendly letter to explain to you the reason the couch in question is where it is. This woman asleep on the couch is dreaming she has been transported into the forest, listening to the sounds from the instrument of the enchanter.

This explanation may be applied to other tropical subjects, particularly those with a female protagonist such as *A Woman Walking in a Forest* and *Unpleasant Surprise*. Renoir saw the latter painting in Ambroise Vollard's shop in 1909 and commented:

It's curious how disconcerted people are

when they confront the qualities of a true painter. The Douanier Rousseau must exasperate them above all others! . . . Isn t is possible to enjoy a painting for the harmony of its colors alone? Is it necessary to understand what it means?

In the last year of his life Rousseau worked day and night at his painting. His reputation was growing beyond France and he was asked by the critic A. Mercereau for three works for an exhibition in Russia. These last months were clouded by his bitter disappointment at his rejection by a widow of 54, who worked in a local shop, and to whom he had proposed marriage and sent gifts he could ill afford. He continued to keep open house on Sunday, the only day in his previous life that he had been able to devote to painting. In an invitation to the President of the Arts Orphanage on 14 June 1910, he explained that:

It is very difficult for me to get away because of my work which at the moment is going well. A Sunday would be easier for me . . . I am at home to guests from 9 to 11 in the morning and from 2.30 to 5.30 after lunch in my studio, an unpretentious and simple working man; but a sincere one.

Rousseau worked throughout August 1910, while most of his friends had left Paris for the annual vacation. He

neglected to treat a cut on his leg, however, and contracted blood poisoning. When he was at last taken to hospital he was beyond help. The only one of his circle of friends left in Paris was Wilhelm Uhde, who visited him. Rousseau died alone on 4 September and the irony and contradictions of his life were compounded at its end by the hospital's diagnosis of the artist as "an alcoholic."

From the pauper's hospital, Rousseau was buried in the pauper's cemetery of Bagneux, where Jarry had been buried three years before. Robert Delaunay and Quéval, Rousseau's landlord from the rue Perrel, bought a 30-year plot in the cemetery, and Apollinaire wrote his epitaph in chalk, lines later chiseled into the gravestone by the Romanian sculptor Constantin Brancusi in 1913, and moved with Rousseau's remains in 1947 to his birthplace, Laval:

We salute you
Gentle Rousseau you hear us
Delaunay his wife Quéval and I
Let our baggage through free at Heaven's gate
We shall bring your brushes, paints and canvas
So that you can devote your sacred leisure in the light of truth
To painting the way you did my portrait
The face of the stars.

LEFT:
Carnival Evening, 1886
Oil on canvas, 46 × 35¼ inches (116.8 × 89.5 cm)
Philadelphia Museum of Art, PA
Louis E. Stern Collection
(63-181-64)

ABOVE:
At the Edge of the Forest, c.1886
Oil on canvas, 27½ × 23¾ inches (70 × 60.5 cm)
Kunsthaus, Zurich

The Toll-House, *c.*1890
Oil on canvas, 16 × 13⅝ inches (40.6 × 32.5 cm)
Courtauld Institute Galleries, London
Courtauld Bequest, 1948

Rendezvous in the Forest, 1889
Oil on canvas, 36¼ × 28¾ inches (92 × 73 cm)
© Board of Trustees, National Gallery of Art, Washington, DC
Gift of the W. Averell Harriman Foundation
in memory of Marie N. Harriman
(1972.9.20 PA)

Myself, Portrait-Landscape, 1890
Oil on canvas, 56¼ × 43⅜ inches (143 × 110 cm)
National Gallery, Prague

Portrait of Pierre Loti, *c.*1891
Oil on canvas, 24½ × 19⅞ inches (62 × 50 cm)
Musée de l'Orangerie, Paris
Photo © RMN

**Tropical Storm with Tiger
(Surprise!),** 1891
Oil on canvas, 51 × 63 inches (130 × 162 cm)
National Gallery, London

34

Artillerymen (Les Artilleurs), *c.*1893-95
Oil on canvas, 31⅛ × 39 inches (79.1 × 98.9 cm)
Solomon R. Guggenheim Museum, New York, NY
Gift, Solomon R. Guggenheim, 1938, Photograph by David Heald ©
The Solomon R. Guggenheim Foundation, New York
(FN 38.711)

The Young Girl (Portrait de Fillette), 1893-95
Oil on canvas, 32 × 26¼ inches (81.3 × 65.6 cm)
Philadelphia Museum of Art, PA
Given by Mr and Mrs R. Sturgis Ingersoll
(38-38-1)

War or the Ride of Discord, 1894
Oil on canvas, 44⅞ × 53⅛ inches (114 × 135 cm)
Musée d'Orsay, Paris
Photo © RMN

The Bièvre at Gentilly, *c.*1895
Oil on canvas, 18 × 21¾ inches (45.9 × 55.2 cm)
Tate Gallery, London

Landscape with Cattle, 1895-1900
Oil on canvas, 20¼ × 26 inches
(51.4 × 66 cm)
Philadelphia Museum of Art, PA
Louis and Walter Arensberg Collection
(50-134-175)

ABOVE:
Bouquet of Flowers, 1895-1900
Oil on canvas, 24 × 19½ inches (61 × 49.5 cm)
Tate Gallery, London

RIGHT:
Portrait of a Woman, Mme M., 1895-97
Oil on canvas, 62¼ × 45¼ inches (158 × 115 cm)
Musée d'Orsay, Paris
Photo © RMN

La Chasse au Tigre (Tiger Hunt), *c.*1895-1904
Oil on canvas, 15 × 18⅛ inches (38.1 × 46 cm)
Columbus Museum of Art, OH
Gift of Ferdinand Howald
(31.91)

The Watermill, *c.*1896
Oil on canvas, 13 × 21⅝ inches (33 × 54.9 cm)
Christies, London

The Cliff, *c.*1896
Oil on canvas, 8⅝ × 13¾ inches (22 × 35 cm)
Musée de l'Orangerie, Paris

Boat in the Storm, after 1896
Oil on canvas, 21¼ × 25⅝ inches (54 × 65 cm)
Musée de l'Orangerie, Paris
Photo © RMN

The Farmyard, 1896-98
Oil on canvas, 9½ × 13 inches (24.1 × 33 cm)
Musée National d'Art Moderne, Paris

The Chair Factory at Alfortville, 1897
Oil on canvas, 28¾ × 36¼ inches (73 × 92 cm)
Musée de l'Orangerie, Paris
Photo © RMN

Self-Portrait with a Lamp, 1900-03
Oil on canvas, 9 × 7½ inches (23 × 19 cm)
Musée du Louvre, Paris, Donation Picasso
Photo © RMN

Portrait of the Second Wife of Rousseau, *c.*1900-03
Oil on canvas, 9 × 7½ inches (23 × 19 cm)
Musée du Louvre, Paris, Donation Picasso
Photo © RMN

ABOVE:
The Artist Painting His Wife, 1900-04
Oil on canvas, 22 × 25⅝ inches (55.9 × 65 cm)
Musée National d'Art Moderne, Paris

RIGHT:
Happy Quartet, *c.*1902
Oil on canvas, 37 × 22½ inches (94 × 57 cm)
Collection of Mrs John Hay Whitney

House on the Outskirts of Paris, *c.*1905
Oil on canvas, 13 × 18¼ inches (33 × 46.4 cm)
The Carnegie Museum of Art, Pittsburgh, PA
Acquired through the generosity of the Sarah Mellon Scaife family
(69.10)

Child with a Puppet, 1903
Oil on canvas, 39⅜ × 31⅞ inches (100 × 81 cm)
Kunstmuseum, Winterthur

ABOVE:
Child with a Doll, 1904-05

Oil on canvas, 26⅜ × 20½ inches (67 × 52 cm)

Musée de l'Orangerie, Paris

Photo © RMN

RIGHT:
The Country Wedding, *c.*1905

Oil on canvas, 67¾ × 44½ inches (172 × 113 cm)

Musée de l'Orangerie, Paris

Photo © RMN

ABOVE:
Woman in Red in the Forest, after 1905
Oil on canvas, 29½ × 23¼ inches (74.9 × 59 cm)
Collection of Paul Guillaume, New York

RIGHT:
Eve, 1905-07
Oil on canvas, 23⅝ × 18⅛ inches (59.9 × 46.1 cm)
Hamburger Kunsthalle

The Pink Candle, 1905-08
Oil on canvas, 6⅜ × 8¾ inches (16.2 × 22.2 cm)
The Phillips Collectiion, Washington, D.C.
Acquired 1930

Merry Jesters: Joyeux Farceurs, *c.*1906
Oil on canvas, 57½ × 44¾ inches (146 × 113.7 cm)
Philadelphia Museum of Art, PA
Louise and Walter Arensberg Collection
(50-134-176)

LEFT:
Liberty Inviting the Artists to Take Part
in the 22nd Salon des Indépendants, 1906
Oil on canvas, 68⅞ × 46½ inches (174.9 × 118.1 cm)
Museum of Modern Art, Tokyo

ABOVE:
Strollers in a Park, 1907-08
Oil on canvas, 18⅛ × 21⅝ inches (46 × 55 cm)
Musée de l'Orangerie, Paris
Photo © RMN

The Snake Charmer, 1907
Oil on canvas, 65 × 73¼ inches (165 × 186 cm)
Musée d'Orsay, Paris
Photo © RMN

Alley in the Park St. Cloud, 1907-08
Oil on canvas, 18⅛ × 14¾ inches (46.2 × 37.6 cm)
Städelsches Kunstinstitut, Frankfurt

The Football Players (Les Joueurs de Football), 1908
Oil on canvas, 39½ × 31⅝ inches (100.5 × 80.3 cm)
Solomon R. Guggenheim Museum, New York, NY
Photograph by David Heald © The Solomon R. Guggenheim
Foundation, New York
(FN 60.1583)

The Jungle: Tiger Attacking a Buffalo, 1908
Oil on canvas, 67¾ × 75⅜ inches (172.1 × 191.5 cm)
© 1995 The Cleveland Museum of Art, OH
Gift of the Hanna Fund
(49.186)

**View of the Bridge at Sèvres
and the Hills at Clamart,
St. Cloud le Bellevue,** 1908
Oil on canvas, 31½ × 40⅛ inches (80 × 102 cm)
Pushkin Museum, Moscow

Battle Between a Buffalo and a Tiger, 1908
Oil on canvas, 18⅛ × 21⅝ inches (46 × 55 cm)
Hermitage Museum, Petersburg

View of Malakoff, Hauts-de-Seine, 1908
Oil on canvas, 16½ × 21⅝ inches (42 × 54.9 cm)
Private Collection

Quay of Ivry, 1908
Oil on canvas, 18 × 21¾ inches (45.9 × 55.2 cm)
Bridgestone Museum of Art, Tokyo

The Fishermen and the Biplane, 1908
Oil on canvas, 18⅛ × 21⅝ inches (46 × 55 cm)
Musée de l'Orangerie, Paris
Photo © RMN

Banks of the Oise, *c.*1908
Oil on canvas, 17¾ × 21⅝ inches (45 × 55 cm)
Smith College Museum of Art, Northampton, MA

Père Juniet's Cart, 1908
Oil on canvas, 38⅛ × 50 inches
(97 × 127 cm)
Musée de l'Orangerie, Paris
Photo © RMN

The Muse Inspiring the Poet, 1908-09
Oil on canvas, 51⅝ × 38⅛ inches (131.2 × 96.9 cm)
Pushkin Museum, Moscow

ABOVE:
The Chair Factory at Alfortville, 1909
Oil on canvas, 15 × 18⅛ inches (38 × 46 cm)
Musée de l'Orangerie, Paris
Photo © RMN

Flowers in a Vase, 1909
Oil on canvas, 17⅞ × 12⅞ inches (45.3 × 32.6 cm)
Albright-Knox Art Gallery, Buffalo, NY
Room of Contemporary Art Fund, 1939

ABOVE:
The Bank of the Bièvre near Bicêtre, 1909
Oil on canvas, 21½ × 18 inches (54.6 × 45.7 cm)
The Metropolitan Museum of Art, New York, NY
Gift of Marshal Field, 1939
(39.15)

The Muse Inspiring the Poet, 1909
Oil on canvas, 77½ × 38⅛ inches (146 × 97 cm)
Kunstmuseum, Basle

ABOVE:
Notre-Dame, 1909
Oil on canvas, 13 × 16 inches (33 × 40.6 cm)
The Phillips Collection, Washington, D.C.

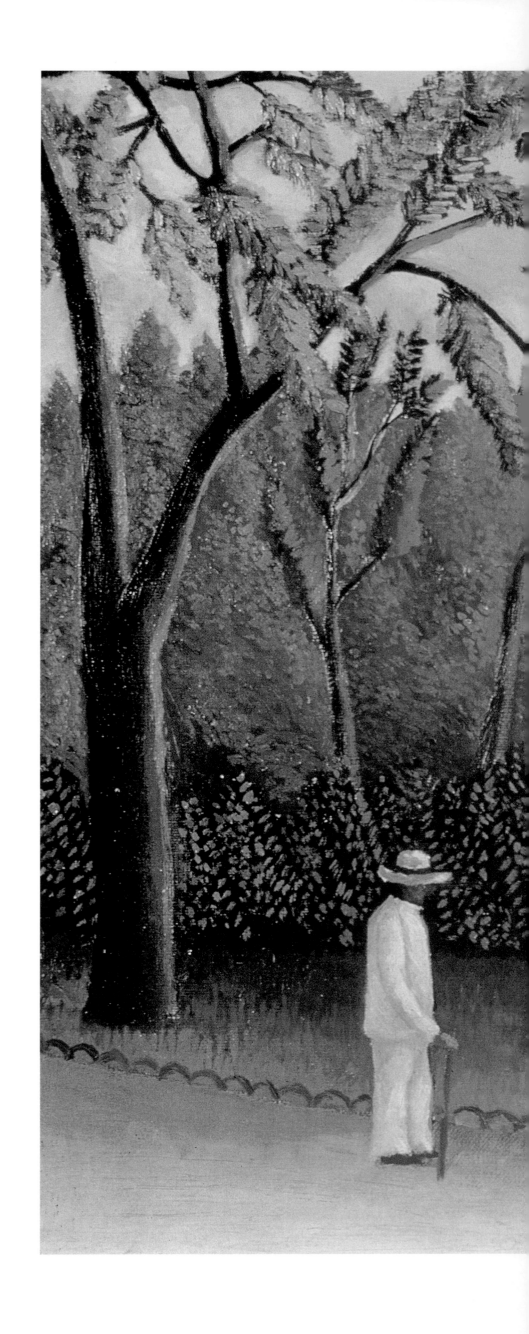

The Luxembourg Garden, 1909
Oil on canvas, 15 × 18⅛ inches (38 × 46 cm)
Hermitage Museum, Petersburg

***Tropical Landscape – An American
Indian Struggling with an Ape,*** 1910
Oil on canvas, 44¾ × 64 inches
(113.6 × 162.5 cm)
*Virginia Museum of Fine Arts, Richmond, VA
Collection of Mr and Mrs Paul Mellon*
(84.3)

Exotic Landscape, 1910
Oil on canvas, 51¼ × 64 inches
(130.2 × 162.6 cm)
Norton Simon Foundation, Pasadena, CA
(F.1971.3.P)

Meadowland, 1910
Oil on canvas, 18 × 21¾ inches (45.9 × 55.2 cm)
Bridgestone Museum of Art, Tokyo

The Waterfall (La Cascade), 1910
Oil on canvas, 45¾ × 59⅛ inches (116.2 × 152.2 cm)
© 1995 *The Art Institute of Chicago, IL*
Helen Birch Bartlett Memorial Collection
(1926.262)

Forest Landscape with Setting Sun, 1910
Oil on canvas, 44⅞ × 64 inches (114 × 162.5 cm)
Kunstmuseum, Basle

A Horse Attacked by a Jaguar, 1910
Oil on canvas, 35⅞ × 45⅝ inches (91 × 115.8 cm)
Pushkin Museum, Moscow

Tropical Forest with Monkeys, 1910
Oil on canvas, 51 × 64 inches
(156.2 × 186.7 cm)
© 1995 Board of Trustees
National Gallery of Art, Washington, D.C.
John Hay Whitney Collection
(1982.76.7, PA)

Acknowledgments

The publisher wishes to thank designer Martin Bristow, picture researchers Suzanne O'Farrell and Sara E. Dunphy, production manager Simon Shelmerdine and editor Jessica Hodge. We should also like to thank the following institutions and agencies for illustrative material.

Albright-Knox Art Gallery, Buffalo, NY: page 92
Archives Larousse-Giraudon: page 7 bottom, 90
The Art Institute of Chicago, IL: pages 9, 11, 104
Bibliothèque Nationale, Paris: pages 13, 23, 24, 25
Bridgeman Art Library, London: pages 8, 42, 49, 50, 78, 82, 96
Bridgestone Museum, Tokyo: pages 84, 102
Carnegie Museum of Art, Pittsburgh, PA: page 58
Cleveland Museum of Art, OH: page 76
Collection of Paul Guillaume, New York: page 62
Collection of Mrs John Hay Whitney: page 57
Columbus Museum of Art, OH: page 48
Courtauld Institute Galleries, London: page 30
Hamburger Kunsthalle: page 63

Kunsthaus, Zurich: pages 27, 33
Kunstmuseum, Basle: pages 94, 106
Kunstmuseum, Winterthur: page 59
Metropolitan Museum of Art, New York, NY: pages 70, 93
Musée des Arts et Traditions Populaires, Paris, photo © RMN: page 17 top
Musée du Louvre, Paris, photo © RMN: pages 22, 41, 54, 55, 72
Musée National d'Art Moderne, Centre Georges Pompidou, Paris: pages 15 bottom, 21 both, 52, 56
Musée de l'Orangerie, Paris, photo © RMN: pages 51, 53, 60, 61, 67, 86, 88, 91
Musée d'Orsay, Paris, photo © RMN: pages 10, 18, 38, 47. 68
Museum of Modern Art, Tokyo: page 66
National Gallery, London: page 34
National Gallery, Prague: pages 12, 32
National Gallery of Art, Washington, D.C.: pages 16, 31, 40, 110

Norton Simon Foundation, Pasadena, CA: page 100
Paris Match: page 19 top
Philadelphia Museum of Art, PA: pages 26, 37, 44, 65
Phillips Collection, Washington D.C.: pages 64, 95
Private Collection: page 19 bottom
Rights reserved: page 20
Roger-Viollet, Paris: pages 6, 7 top, 14, 15 top, 17 bottom
Scala, Florence: pages 80, 108
Setagaya Museum, Tokyo: page 28
Smith College Museum of Art, Northampton, MA: page 87
Solomon R. Guggenheim Museum, New York, NY: pages 36, 75
Städelsches Kunstinstitut, Frankfurt: page 74
Tate Gallery, London: page 46
Virginia Museum of Fine Arts, Richmond, VA: page 98